at **Work** *series*

D1649221

INTERNATIONAL HEAVY TRUCKS

of the 1950s

Ron Adams

Iconografix

Iconografix
PO Box 446
Hudson, Wisconsin 54016 USA

Library of Congress Control Number: 2005936377

ISBN-13: 978-1-58388-160-6
ISBN-10: 1-58388-160-3

06 07 08 09 10 11 6 5 4 3 2 1

Printed in China

Cover and book design by Dan Perry

Copyediting by Suzie Helberg

Cover photo- An "S" series for Utter-Anderson Distributing Co. of Jackson, Michigan. This one delivered great tasting Old Milwaukee beer. Although we see cast spoke wheels on this model, the heavier versions most likely used disc wheels. *Ron Adams Collection*

BOOK PROPOSALS

Iconografix is a publishing company specializing in books for transportation enthusiasts. We publish in a number of different areas, including Automobiles, Auto Racing, Buses, Construction Equipment, Emergency Equipment, Farming Equipment, Railroads & Trucks. The Iconografix imprint is constantly growing and expanding into new subject areas.

Authors, editors, and knowledgeable enthusiasts in the field of transportation history are invited to contact the Editorial Department at Iconografix, Inc., PO Box 446, Hudson, WI 54016.

DEDICATION

Anyone who drove our highways back in the 1950s knew that there were a lot of trucks sharing the highways with you. Anyone who knew something about trucks could tell that many of the trucks that traveled the highways were International trucks, from the small pickups to the big RDF-405s. Almost every International truck had a different driver who should receive recognition for the job they have done. I congratulate all of those drivers who did their jobs well, but there are four drivers that I would like to give special recognition to who also drove International trucks. They are my four uncles:

Kenny Boyer (deceased) started driving truck at the age of 15. He started with a 1938 Ford tractor-trailer hauling potatoes for Edna Sechler. After a few years he left that job and started driving for Paul Levan who owned a few trucks in the local area. The first truck he drove for this man was a D-40, after that a KB-8 and an R-200. In 1956, he left this job and started driving for Nothstein Bros. There he drove an R-200, a V-8 series, and finished off his career in a Mack until his retirement. Edna Sechler and Paul Levan were located in the town of Wanamakers. Nothstein Bros. was located in Trexlertown. Both were towns in Pennsylvania.

William "Billy" Boyer (deceased) started driving in the late 1940s. His first job was driving for Paul C. Miller Trucking Inc. of Orefield, Pennsylvania. There he drove a KB-8 and a KB-10. For a short time after that he drove milk trucks locally for Arthur Snyder of Allentown, Pennsylvania. He also drove for Nothstein Bros. of Trexlertown in 1959, driving an R-200.

After a few years he left there and drove a "U" model Mack for General Seating Co. in Topton, Pennsylvania, until he passed away in 1975. His driving for Paul C. Miller Trucking Inc. was to Virginia and in the states surrounding Pennsylvania.

Arlan "Dutch" Miller (deceased) started driving in 1952 for a local milk hauler, Loch Bros., who took over the milk hauling operation of Arthur Snyder who was previously mentioned. He started driving in an R-170, then a GMC with an automatic transmission, and then a "B" series International. After leaving there, he started working for Penn Dot where the dump trucks he drove were Internationals. There he did whatever kind of hauling was needed and also did snow plowing.

Stanley "Whitey" Miller (living) started driving for Paul Levan in 1952. He drove a KB-7 dump truck. After a few years he then started driving for Wallace Becker in Allentown, Pennsylvania, where he drove an L-184 single axle dump truck and an L-190 ten-wheeler dump truck. Then in 1959 he drove for Nothstein Bros. in an RF-190. After a few years he gave up driving and looked for other types of employment.

My uncles' driving was mostly local driving and they drove mostly Internationals, driving on the same roads that their fellow over-the-road truck drivers drove on. The four of them did their jobs and did them well. I dedicate this book on International trucks to my four uncles Kenny, Billy, Dutch, and Whitey. Those good memories were made and not forgotten.

INTRODUCTION

Cyrus McCormick and Henry Weber never thought that they would go into the history books among other famous American inventors. But that is what happened after Cyrus McCormick invented the reaper and Henry Weber started his Wagon Works. McCormick continued to invent other implements that helped to make farming easier. Weber produced a quality line of wagons for many different types of uses for different parts of the country. Both McCormick and Weber enjoyed success in both of their ventures.

As the end of the 1800s approached, the motor truck had been developed right along with the motorcar. Two men, one for McCormick and one for Deering, each built their own passenger cars. After viewing each of them with their bosses, neither of them was too enthused with the idea.

Then, in 1902, both McCormick and Deering merged their companies. After the merger, the new company was known as The International Harvester Co. Before the merger, farmers were the customers of both companies. International Harvester's first farm tractor was produced in 1906 with their first truck to follow in 1907. It was known as the "Auto Buggy" or "High Wheeler." In 1907, 100 were produced and the idea took on so strong that a plant was built in Akron, Ohio, where production reached 1,000 units per year. The "High Wheelers" were produced until 1916. Internationals then took on a new look with the sloped hood and the radiator behind the engine, it had a similar look as the Renault. This appearance lasted until 1923. After this, many different models came and went—models like the "S" of the 1920s, the "AA," "C," and "D" of the 1930s, then the "K," "KB," "W," and the "L" series of the 1940s.

After World War II truck production really took off because during the war only one out of every ten trucks went for commercial use, which created a shortage of trucks. Those that existed during the war were so worn out from constant use that a "take parts from Peter and put on Paul" scenario was taking shape in order to keep trucks running so the trucking companies could survive. This left many idle trucks. After the war there was then a surplus of military trucks, which some companies purchased in order to survive until a fleet of new ones could be obtained. New models were designed, such as the "W" series of 1947, along with a little changing of the prewar "K" model into the "KB" series. The new "KB" series had more chrome externally. The "KB" model was a very popular and widely used truck in every field of trucking. The "W" series was designed for Western trucking.

In 1949, the "KB" was replaced by the new "L" series, along with the new "Metro" for local door-to-door customers. The "KB" was still being produced in 1949. In the 1950s the "KB" models were eliminated. The new LD-300 and LD-400 conventionals and the LDC-400 cab over engine replaced the "W" series. The "L" series was slightly redesigned and became the new "R" series in 1953. The R-190 and R-200 series continued on through the 1950s. In 1955 the "S" series and the "CO" low cab over engine series were produced. The

LCD cab over engine of the early 1950s and the RDC-405 cab over engine were known as the International "Cherry Pickers" because of the high sitting cabs.

In 1956 the new "V" series was introduced along with the "VCO" series low cab over engine. Also in 1956, a new flat front cab over engine was designed and was known as the DCO-405 series Emeryville. This was probably the most popular over-the-road model for International. In 1957, the "A" series, "AC" series, and the "ACO" cab over engine series, known as the Sightliner, were introduced. I might add that the DCO-405 Emeryville replaced the RDC-405 cab over engine. The "A" and the "AC" series lasted only two years and were then replaced by the "B" and "BC" series in 1959. The "Pay Hauler" off-highway dump truck was also introduced in 1959. Some of the 1950s models continued into the 1960s.

In 1950-51 the Federal Government laid out plans to build a new highway system known as the Interstate Highway System. This would be a network of highways from coast to coast that would bypass towns and big cities to make traveling easier and a lot faster, although it was not fully completed until the early 1970s.

What did this highway network mean to the trucking industry? It meant that goods could be shipped a lot faster instead of having to go through towns and cities with stop-and-go traffic. This brought on changes for truck manufacturers including International. In the mid-to-late 1950s, 40-foot trailers were becoming legal. There were states that allowed only 50-foot legal lengths. So International designed tractors with short enough wheelbases and BBCs to pull these 40-foot trailers legally, with both conventional and cab over engine models. The weight limits also increased. With this came the demand for more powerful engines. In 1956, International discontinued using Buda and Hall-Scott engines and only offered Cummins Diesels. In the late 1950s and early 1960s horsepower in the engines had increased to as high as 335. This was largely due to the development of the 97-foot turnpike trains, which was one tractor pulling two 40-foot trailers, which meant pulling double the weight. These were seen on the Ohio, Indiana, and Massachusetts turnpikes and the New York State thruway.

International trucks were so popular that through the 1950s a total of more than 1,283,000 vehicles were sold. This included school buses, military vehicles, bottom-dump wagons for construction, payscrapers, and duo-pactors. All other kinds of vehicles were used in all kinds of work from small pickups on the farm to the big off-highway and oilfield trucks.

They did it all. They came in all sizes; small, medium, large, and extra-large. It's safe to say that if International could not make it, it could not be made.

As you view the selection of photographs in this book, you will see most of the different models in different configurations doing all kinds of work and some of the many customers that used International trucks.

This shot shows a fleet of Model L-180s that were in the city pickup and delivery fleet at the St. Louis, Missouri, terminal for Roadway Express Inc. of Akron, Ohio. The L-180 used cast spoke wheels. *P. R. Papin Photo Co.*

When things needed to be kept cold, ice blocks and ice cubes were the answer. The F&F Ice and Cube Service in the Bronx, New York, came to the rescue with this Model L-181, which used disc wheels. The L-180 models used Super Blue Diamond 269 engines. *George Salkin Associates Inc.*

The Model L-180 was also available in tractor form. This one was in the fleet of Interstate Motor Freight System of Grand Rapids, Michigan, pulling a Fruehauf trailer. Again, notice the cast spoke wheels. *Neil Sherff*

Here we have another L-180 model but this time with a sleeper cab. The tractors also used the Super Blue Diamond 269 engines. Interstate Motor Freight System of Grand Rapids, Michigan, is the company that it worked for. *Neil Sherff*

The Model L-200 was introduced in 1950. It was known as the Roadliner. The standard engine was the Super Red Diamond 406. It worked for the Northwestern Glass Co. of Seattle, Washington, and pulled a Fruehauf trailer. *Ron Adams Collection*

Here we have an L-190 with a tandem axle. The Super Red Diamond 450 engine was used in the 190 series. The 190 also used cast spoke wheels. This one was in the fleet of Wheeler Transport Service of Menasha, Wisconsin, and pulled a Trailmobile tanker trailer. *Ron Adams Collection*

This new model added to the line was the LC cab over engine that was known as the Emeryville. The high cab was also known as the "Cherry Picker" International. This LTCD-405 was owned by the American Finishing Co. of Siluria, Alabama, and is seen here pulling a Brown trailer. The available engines were Cummins, Buda, and Hall-Scott. Nine Fuller and Spicer transmissions were also available. *Ron Adams Collection*

Doubles were always a popular combination in the western states. This Model LCD-405 was used to pull this set of Brown doubles for Charles R. Hart Transportation Co. based in California. *Ron Adams Collection*

The heaviest non-western truck was the L-200. The standard engine for this one was the Super Red Diamond 406. This L-200, pulling a Brown open-top trailer, was in the fleet of Mid-states Freight Lines Inc. of Chicago, Illinois. Notice that the turn signals are mounted on the bumper guides. *International Harvester*

The LD-400 series was the axle forward model. This early 1950s version was set up as a truck-trailer combination for hauling lumber. The LD-400 series was the take-over model of the W series from the 1940s. The engines offered were Cummins, Buda, and Hall-Scott. This was most likely a 1950 or 1951 model because of the small rearview mirrors. *Ron Adams Collection*

Another LD-400 series is this one at work for McLaughlin Trucking of Chicago, Illinois. Its partner is a Tec dump trailer. Again we see the small rearview mirrors. Nine Fuller and Spicer transmissions were available. *Joe Wanchura*

Here we have another LD-400 that was still used in the very early 1960s, judging from the cars it's hauling. The carrier is unknown. Every vehicle on the load is different. *Ron Adams Collection*

The LD-300 series was the set back front axle version. When this picture was taken is anybody's guess, but we do know that it was taken after 1,000,000 miles had been driven. The truck was used in the Transport Division for the Cassiar Asbestos Corp. of White-horse, Yukon Territory. Chains were a must when traveling the Alaska Highway. Notice that behind the truck is a D-400 series tractor, circa 1962. *Ron Adams Collection*

From the looks of this tractor, it is possible that this one was an LFC-420, which was rated at 70,000 pounds. Notice the extension to the frame and the stack going up through the hood. The two round pipes on the front are probably for the grille guard. The tractor is set up to pull the big high tonnage dump trailer for Open Mining Hauling. *Ron Adams Collection*

This L-195 was working for Emery Transportation Co. of Chicago, Illinois. The power source was the Super Red Diamond 406-cubic-inch engine. The L-190 series had the standard small rearview mirror but the driver made a switch to the bigger West Coast type mirrors and also added fender mount rearview mirrors. Coming up behind is a Fruehauf stainless steel trailer. *Neil Sherff*

The Malarkey Company owned this L-190. The power source on this model was the Super Red Diamond 372-cubic-inch engine. The wheelbase ranged from 133 up to 193 inches. This is one of several different types of trucks in the fleet of the Oregon-based carrier. *Ron Adams Collection*

In this cab over engine series, the lighter weight models had three horizontal bars whereas the heavier weight models had four bars. Also, the lighter models had disc wheels and the heavier models had cast spoke wheels. Southway Freight Service of Seattle, Washington, owned the truck. *Ron Adams Collection*

Although this is an L series, it shows the four horizontal bars representing the heavier tractor. The owner is Sam Izzo Co. of Saginaw, Michigan. Notice the West Coast mirrors and the sun visor. The trailer is a Fruehauf made of stainless steel. *Neil Sherff*

Here we have the lighter weight R-series tractor. Notice the three horizontal bars. The tractor is pulling a Trailmobile trailer. The rig is owned by Miratile Manufacturing Co. of Elkhart, Indiana. *Neil Sherff*

In 1953, the new R line was introduced. The light and medium duty model received a facelift. Here we see an R-180 of the new design. This was the first year of the new "IH" emblem on all the trucks, replacing the three-diamond emblem. Northwestern Glass Company of Seattle, Washington, owns the tractor. The trailer is a Fruehauf "Aerovan." *Ron Adams Collection*

This is the R-190 of the heavier weight models. This series was introduced in 1952. The change from the "L" to the "R" series was that the "L" had seven vertical bars in the grille whereas the "R" went down to three bars. The standard engine in the R-190 was International's RD-406 gasoline six. This R-190 is set up as a tandem axle straight truck that was owned by the Quaker Oats Company of St. Joseph, Missouri. *Bray Studio*

The next bigger model was the ever-so-popular R-200. This model also used the International RD-406 gasoline six engine. The owner of this tractor chose the optional sleeper cab. The shortest wheelbase for a sleeper cab was 157 inches. The owner added a grille guard and a roadlight rack. The swan goes flying high down the road for Middle Atlantic Transportation Co. Inc. of Bridgeport, Connecticut, who the truck is leased to. *Neil Sherff*

Here we have another 200 series tractor, but this time as an RD-200 diesel tandem. A Cummins Diesel, probably a JBS-600, according to the specification sheet, powered this one. The truck is owned by L. E. Boling of Kewanee, Illinois, and is pulling a Martin lowbed trailer to haul a huge dozer. Notice that on top of the cab there are three cab lights in each corner. The reason for this is unknown. The three lights could be warning lights for nighttime driving with an oversized load. Also notice the Mack Bulldog hood ornament. *Ron Adams Collection*

Earlier we featured a truck for Cassiar Asbestos Corp. in a tandem axle version. Here we have another truck for the same company, an RD-300 in a single axle version. The standard engine was a Cummins HRB-600. The trailer is a custom built Fruehauf Dura-Van. The chains are a necessity for Yukon Territory driving. *Ron Adams Collection*

This RDFC-405 is circa 1953. The standard engine in this model was the Cummins HRB-600. It was known as the "Emeryville." The cab had a flat floor with no "doghouse." The wheelbases varied from 128 to 212 inches. Hartz Mountain Products Corp. of New York, Chicago, and Los Angeles owned the rig. *Neil Sherff*

This RDTC-405 is a rather short wheelbase. As we see in this picture, an add-on sleeper box was added. The reason for this setup is because, if a full sleeper cab was used, no reefer trailer could be pulled. With the add-on sleeper box in the low position, a reefer trailer could be pulled with the reefer unit clearing both the cab and sleeper box. These cabs sit a lot higher than most. Navajo Freight Lines Inc., at this time, was located in Albuquerque, New Mexico. *Navajo Freight Lines*

The Auburn Lumber Co. in Auburn, California, delivered building materials to new home projects in and around the Auburn area. Here we see an L-160 making a delivery of shingles. The body was raised, which made it easier to get the shingle packs to the roof rather than shoulder transport them up a ladder. Notice the signal arm on the cab, which was rather unusual for this model. *Auburn Lumber Co.*

Here we see a Michigan style gravel train being pulled by an RDF-300. The standard engine was a Cummins HRB-600 Diesel. The trains of the 1950s did not have as many axles as those of the 1960s. *Neil Sherff*

The R-190 was a very popular model. The standard engine was the RD-406 gasoline six, but an optional engine was the RD-450 gasoline six. A sleeper cab was also an option. Western Auto Supply Co. in Taunton, Massachusetts, decided on this day to pull the new Fruehauf volume van trailer. *Ron Adams Collection*

This RD-220 was busy hauling freight for H. R. Cook Truck Line of Springdale, Arkansas, in the Trailmobile trailer. The driver enjoyed the comfort of a sleeper cab to rest in on those Arkansas to Michigan runs, the latter is where the picture was taken. Again, the standard engine was a Cummins HRB-600. A 157-inch wheelbase was the shortest allowed with a sleeper cab. *Neil Sherff*

Pulling double trailers required a tractor with a short enough wheelbase to stay within the legal length limit. This RDC-405 fit the bill. The standard engine was a Cummins HRB-600 Diesel. The tractor is working for Pacific Motor Trucking Co. pulling trailers for Southern Pacific Truck Service, a division of the Southern Pacific Railroad. *Ron Adams Collection*

The Santa Fe Trail Transportation Co. of Wichita, Kansas, was the trucking division of the Santa Fe Railroad. This RDTC-405 tractor was one of several for over-the-road work and pulled a Brown trailer. The rear axle was a dead axle with 55 percent load on the drive and 45 percent load on the dead axle. The power source is the Cummins HRB-600. *Santa Fe Trail Transportation Co.*

In 1954 there was a new addition to the over-the-road line. It was the CO series. This 190 was kept busy hauling Dickies clothes in the Trailmobile trailer coast to coast. Wheelbases ranged from 99 up to 153 inches. The standard engine was the Super Red Diamond 372 cubic inch. The standard wheels were cast spoke but this customer chose optional disc wheels instead. *Bill Wood photo*

Introduced in 1953 was the RD series, which was the continuation of the L series. This RDC-405 was one in a fleet that belonged to Schumacher Motor Express, based in Eau Claire, Wisconsin. They operated between Chicago and St. Paul. A Cummins Diesel or a Hall-Scott were the engine choices available. This customer chose standard cast spoke wheels. *International Harvester Co.*

The RD-400 series was a popular truck for the heavy haulers. This one is set up for oilfield work in Alaska. Many chains were needed for tying down and securing loads. Notice the front guard to protect the front end. Homer Freight Lines of Anchorage, Alaska, is the hauler. *Ron Adams Collection*

This RDC-405 came into the P-I-E fleet in 1954, one of a large fleet that was ordered. These were of lightweight aluminum. They were used east of Denver in the P-I-E system. A Cummins JT-6-B Diesel engine was used to replace the large NHB-600. The 140-inch wheelbase gave a GCW (gross capacity weight) of 68,000 pounds. The sleeper cab had to be made shorter, lowered 8 inches, and moved forward 2 inches to allow 35-foot trailers to go straight through from the Pacific Coast to Chicago without having to reload in Denver. A couple inches per tractor meant substantial savings to a company like P-I-E. *P-I-E*

Eastern Motor Express Inc. of Terre Haute, Indiana, operated from Chicago and St. Louis on their west end and to the East Coast on the east end. A variety of Internationals were among the fleet. One of those was this R-200 tandem axle pulling this Fruehauf stainless steel open-top trailer. The standard engine was the RD-406 gasoline six. *Eastern Motor Express*

The three big steel coils were the load of the day on this trip, but were no problem for this RDF-210. The engine was the Cummins HRB-600 Diesel that powered this Michigan style steel rig down the highway. It was owned by Perry Stenen and leased to Brada Cartage Co. of Kokomo, Indiana. *Neil Sherff*

The RDF-320 is the heaviest of the set back front axle series. This one was set up to work in the oilfields. The power came from the Cummins HRB-600 Diesel. Optional engines were a Buda or a Hall-Scott Butane. The radiator guard and headlight guard are optional. *Ron Adams Collection*

Associated Grocers in Seattle, Washington, had these two R-180s doing local delivery work in and around Seattle. The bodies are Aero-Liner reefers. *Peter Clarke photographer*

This CO model was introduced in 1954 and continued up until 1972. The CO-200 used the Super Red Diamond 406 engine. Highway Freight Inc. of Newark, New Jersey, was the owner of this CO-200 that pulled the flatbed that is loaded with lumber. Notice that there are no chains, ropes, or straps used to tie down the load. *Highway Transport*

Another CO model, this time doing sanitary waste service somewhere in Dade County, Florida. This is one of 12 trucks used by Michael Bunetta for Industrial Waste Disposal Service. Notice that this one is diesel powered. The refuse body is built by Leach. *Ron Adams Collection*

This 1955 picture shows an RD-300 pulling a set of bulk feed or bulk cement trailers in Michigan. The engine was a Cummins HRB-600 Diesel. The company is unknown. *Neil Sherff*

The CO-190 was also available in a tandem axle version, as we see here. The standard engine is the Super Red Diamond 372. Messingers in Cedar Rapids, Iowa, owns the tractor and the Transport trailer that is hauling the Link-Belt shovel. *Transport Trailers*

Richard Guerra of Middlebury, Connecticut, loved restoring vintage trucks back to their original looks. This 1955 RDCOF-405 is a perfect example of the restoration work that he does. He decided to use optional disc wheels and a modern day fuel tank, and also air horns and cab lights. *Ron Adams Collection*

Here we see another RDF-405 with a day cab and an add-on box sleeper. The power source was the popular Cummins HRB-600 Diesel. The truck was owned by the American Meter Co. of Philadelphia, Pennsylvania, and pulled a Trailmobile trailer. The customer chose the optional disc wheels. *Neil Sherff*

When Mr. Gary Johnson decided that he wanted to restore a truck, he picked this 1955 RDF-405 and a 1963 Aero-Liner reefer trailer. It was a very good choice and a very super restoration job. The power comes from a Cummins Diesel. The color scheme and its chrome make this rig look super nice. *Don Mackenzie*

Seeing these big RD-400s was an awesome sight, and driving one of them was probably equally awesome. These cabs had a straight floor with no doghouse to deal with. A Cummins HRB-600 Diesel engine provided the power that was needed to haul the freight in the ventilated Trailmobile trailer. *Ron Adams Collection*

This is an RDC-405. This truck and many others like it were seen in the southern states for Great Southern Trucking Co. of Jacksonville, Florida. These single axle tractors also used the Cummins HRB-600 Diesel. They also could use the optional Hall-Scott gasoline engine or a Buda diesel. This company's name was later changed to Ryder Truck Lines Inc. The trailer is a Miller. *Ron Adams Collection*

The new S-line was brought into the lineup in 1955. This style only existed for two years through 1956. This S-180 is working for Shippers Dispatch Inc. of South Bend, Indiana, pulling a Fruehauf open-top trailer. Four gasoline engines were available in this model. The first was a Blue Diamond 269 and the other three were the Black Diamond 264, 282, and 308. The photo was taken in 1957 in Detroit. *Neil Sherff*

A number of carriers that ran up the East Coast were southern companies. One of these companies was Harper Motor Lines Inc. of Elberton, Georgia. The decal on the front was a dead giveaway that a Cummins Diesel, probably the HRB-600, powered the truck. The cargo was being hauled in a Fruehauf volume van trailer. *Robert J. Parrish*

The sign on the trailer reads "100 Years—Quality & Service." The Robinson Clay Products Co., location unknown, boasted about their product and used this CO model and rack side trailer to haul their product. The West Coast type mirrors were probably an option, versus the small rectangle mirrors. *Neil Sherff*

Many carriers had divisions separate from the regular freight division. Yellow Transit Freight Lines Inc. of Indianapolis, Indiana, was one of those carriers. Here we see a CO model with a tandem axle pulling a spread axle flatbed trailer loaded with steel coils for Yellow Transit's Steel Division. Jim Leavitt owns the tractor. *Neil Sherff*

The R-190 was used in every type of trucking. This one happens to be in a tank truck operation and is seen here pulling a Butler spread axle petroleum tank trailer for Producers Transport Inc. of New Buffalo, Michigan. The engine was the RD-406 gasoline engine. *Ron Adams Collection*

This S-182 was a good truck for farm work. This one has a combination grain and stock body. Standard wheelbases went from 130 to 172 inches. The standard engine was the 308-cubic-inch Black Diamond. *International Harvester*

A heavier tractor model was this one for Chicago, Michigan, and Eastern Freight Lines Inc. of Chicago, Illinois, pulling a rack side trailer for hauling steel. It wasn't one of the most powerful tractors but it got the job done the same as the rest. *Neil Sherff*

A tractor in the R line that was rarely seen was the RD-205 super space saver. The BBC was shortened a full 12 inches. Roadway Express Inc. of Akron, Ohio, chose to purchase a large fleet of these with the Cummins JT-6-B six-cylinder turbocharged Diesel engines with 5-speed transmissions. This photo was taken in Detroit in 1958. *Neil Sherff*

A new addition to the lineup in 1956 was the new V series. This V-210 was hauling a load of steel for the photo shoot. The 461-cubic-inch V-8 was the only engine offered. This one has the new style turn signals. *International Harvester*

This VT-195 is seen here doing duty pulling a gasoline tank trailer for Kampo Transit Inc. of Neenah, Wisconsin. The standard engine was the V-401 eight-cylinder Y-block. The wheelbases ranged from 133 to 193 inches. A sleeper cab was optional. *Neil Sherff*

This CO-190 was a short wheelbase tractor. Although the exact wheelbase is unknown, the shortest offered was 99 inches. Sleeper cabs were offered as special equipment. This CO-190 pulled a Heil Tank Trailer in the bulk hauling division for Olson Transportation Co. of Green Bay, Wisconsin. *Olson Transportation*

The introduction of the CO series in 1954 turned into the VCO series in 1956. Here we see two VCOF-190s. The standard engine was the small 401 cubic inch. These two VCOF-190s probably had the big V-461 engine. The GVWs of these ranged from 30,000 to 41,000 pounds for a GCW of 62,000 pounds. Berman Leasing Co. owned the rigs and they were on lease with American Can Co. Highway trailers carried the freight. *Shaner Studios, Pottstown, Pennsylvania*

This FC-402-L was welcomed by the construction industry. Instead of having a separate engine behind the cab, this truck had the PTO in the front of the truck engine, which allowed the main engine to turn the 6-1/2-cubic-yard cement drum. The engine was the Red Diamond 450 gas engine that put out 182 horsepower. The "L" designated that many aluminum components were used. Pacific Coast Aggregates owned the truck. *Ron Adams Collection*

The year 1956 brings on another new series known as the CD series. Its appearance is similar to the RD cab over line. The fender lost the skirt from behind the front wheel and became a straight fender. This DC-405 has the optional sleeper cab, and is probably Cummins powered. It's seen here pulling a Black Diamond trailer for Bush Transfer Co. Inc. of Lenoir, North Carolina. *Robert J. Parrish*

This DFC-405 and Fruehauf trailer belongs to a food products company. A wide range of Cummins Diesels were available from 165 up to 300 horsepower. A Hall-Scott gas engine was also available. Both Fuller and Spicer transmissions were also available. Cast spoke wheels were fitted on this tractor with disc wheels as an option. This one chose the add-on sleeper box instead of a sleeper cab. *Ron Adams Collection*

Garrett Freightlines Inc. of Pocatello, Idaho, covered 11 western states. Various types and makes of equipment were used throughout their system. One was this DC-405 pulling behind a set of Williamsen double trailers. On this tractor Garrett chose the optional disc wheels and also added an optional set of sanders. *Garrett Freightlines Inc.*

Of all the cab over engine models that International produced, there is no question that the new style DCO series Emeryville was the most popular of all. This DCO-405 had the 50-inch cab, which allowed it to pull double 25-foot trailers and reach the 60-foot legal length. A Cummins Diesel was the standard engine. Two other cab sizes were available with 72- or 80-inch sleeper cabs. Tractor number 6044 was owned by So-Cal (Southern California) Freight Lines Inc. of Palo Alto, California, and pulled a set of Fruehauf double trailers. *So-Cal Freight Lines*

International, like other manufacturers, made some strange configurations—at the customers' demands, of course. This tractor was made at the Emeryville plant. It was designed with the 50-inch cab to add a 20-foot dromedary body on a 310-inch wheelbase to pull a 35-foot trailer at the 60-foot length. This added up to 55 feet of cargo space. The engine used in this setup was an inline six 779-cubic-inch 190 Hall-Scott similar to the "pancake" Cummins. Although no name is shown here the customer could have been P-I-E. *International Harvester*

Here we have a DCOF-405 for Kampo Transit Inc. of Neenah, Wisconsin. This is the standard tractor with cast spoke wheels and 70-inch cab. The brand name of this trailer is unknown but the cargo is milk. Notice the Chicago Board of Health permit on the trailer. *Kampo Transit Inc.*

This RDF-405 was one in a large fleet for Southern Pacific Truck Service of San Francisco, California. It is set up as a truck-trailer combination with tank body and trailer for hauling gasoline. The year 1956 was the midway point for the existence of this big RD-400 series. *Southern Pacific Truck Service*

Another Southern Pacific piece of equipment was this DC-405 short wheelbase tractor. Its purpose was for pulling double trailers. This tractor features optional disc wheels. *Southern Pacific Truck Service*

Another in this series is the DCF-405. The wheelbases ranged from 141 to 212 inches, therefore allowing this unit to be set up as a truck-trailer combination. The power came from a Cummins Diesel. By this time Hall-Scott and Buda engines were no longer offered. Shown are the optional disc wheels. Due to the type of cargo being hauled the body cross frames are steel instead of wood. Concrete Conduit Co. of Colton, California, was the private hauler. *Ron Adams Collection*

Since 1928, Pyramid Van Lines Inc. of Cleveland, Ohio, was moving people from here to there and everywhere. Of course, at that time the Emeryvilles did not exist, but some 38 years later they were available. This DCO-405 had the optional 80-inch cab with the standard cast spoke wheels. The tractor was owned by Lenny and leased to Pyramid Van Lines Inc. It is seen here pulling a Reliance moving van trailer. *Alvin M. Stuller photography*

This DCOF-405, which was unit No. 1 for Merriman Transfer of Merriman, Nebraska, is pulling a Wilson Livestock trailer. The trailer is about 50 feet long. The cast spoke wheels are standard but the 80-inch sleeper cab is optional. This photo was taken at the Wilson Trailer plant in Sioux City, Iowa. *Woodworth Commercial Photos*

Here we see a longer than normal wheelbase for a single axle tractor. This DCO-405 was hauling for Dairyland Milk Foods pulling an unknown brand name milk tanker trailer. Again, it had the standard cast spoke wheels and 72-inch cab. The sanders are optional. There is no shortage of fenders and mud flaps on this rig. *Williams Bros. photographers*

This big D-400 series tractor stands tall as it pulls the Great Dane reefer trailer behind. The carrier is unknown but it could likely be a southern hauler. The fenders were hinged to swing out for easy access to the side of the engine. To work on top of the engine, the passenger's seat and floorboard could be removed in less than a minute. The Cummins Diesel engine was installed at a 20-degree tilt. *Neil Sherff*

This style of cab with the shorter fenders only existed in 1956. This style was the forerunner of the famous model known as the Emeryville. Western Express Inc. of Cleveland, Ohio, operated this DC-405. The trailer is a Fruehauf that is owned by Mid-American Truck Lines Inc. of Kansas City, Missouri. This combination was known as Inter-lining. The tractor had an optional add-on sleeper box. *Neil Sherff*

The DCO series was introduced in 1956. Here we see a DCO-405 for So-Cal Freight Lines Inc., of Los Angeles, California, pulling a combo of triple trailers in the Defense Transportation Parade on June 20, 1957, in Monterey, California. This tractor had the 50-inch cab. By 1956, Hall-Scott and Buda engines were no longer available in International trucks. The only choice was a Cummins Diesel. Optional disc wheels were the customer's choice. *Allied Photography*

In 1957 a brand new cab over engine was introduced. The new model was the ACO Sightliner. Two sizes of cabs were offered: a 48-inch and a 72-inch sleeper cab. The Sightliner had a triple windshield that afforded better visibility. Three V-8 engines were offered: a V-401, a V-461, and a V-549. The wheelbases went from 98 inches up to 140 inches. This photo shows a good view of the front triple windshield. This tractor is pulling a set of double flatbed trailers. The carrier is unknown. *Neil Sherff*

This side view shows the short 48-inch cab and the short wheelbase. Notice that each of the two lower windows has windshield wipers. Tractor number 3 was owned by Arvil K. Woodruff and leased to Rawling Sporting Goods of St. Louis, Missouri. *Neil Sherff*

Another Sightliner is this one for Peerless Distributing Co. of Detroit, Michigan. It's pulling a set of double tank trailers. This photograph was taken in March 1959 near Fowlerville, Michigan. *Neil Sherff*

Another brand new model was the "A" series. This A-170 featured the sleeper cab. The standard engine was the Black Diamond with 282 cubic inches. The Chevalley Moving and Storage Co. in Oklahoma was the agent for Mayflower Transit Co. Inc. The trailer is a Trailmobile. *Neil Sherff*

Another "A" series is this A-170. This one has a day cab and is pulling a Fruehauf trailer for Fruit Belt Motor Service of Chicago, Illinois. The appearance of this series is similar to the "S" series of 1956. *Neil Sherff*

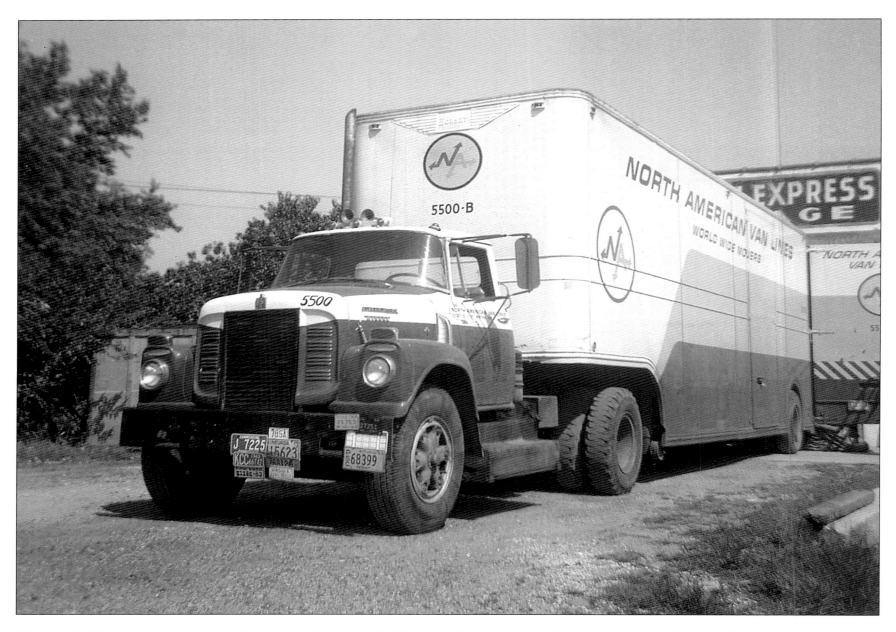

The new "A" line changed entirely from the 1/2-ton to 33,000 pounds. Wraparound windshield, and fenders that faired into the door panels, eliminated the running boards. This AC Diesel probably has the cast spoke wheels as standard equipment. The tractor is pulling a Dorsey moving van trailer for North American Van Lines of Ft. Wayne, Indiana. *Harry Patterson*

Still another new model in the lineup was the "AC" series. The standard engine was the Cummins NH-180 Diesel. The cab on the AC was 6 inches shorter than the super space saver cab used on the "R" series. The 90-inch BBC allowed these rigs to pull 40-foot trailers. The Battle Creek Box Co. of Battle Creek, Michigan, is the owner of the rig. *Neil Sherff*

This AC-220 was fitted with a sleeper cab. It is seen here pulling two flatbed trailers for hauling steel. It was in the steel division for Gateway Transportation Co. of La Crosse, Wisconsin. This picture was taken in Detroit in 1959. *Neil Sherff*

The RD-220 had the Cummins HRB-600 Diesel engine, the Comfo-Vision cab, and cast spoke wheels as standard equipment. Stoll Packing Corp. of New York City, New York, used this tractor and Fruehauf reefer trailer to run between New York and Chicago. *Neil Sherff*

The R series came along in 1953. The appearance of this R series did not change much. This R-220 was owned by the Hobbs Trailer Co. of Fort Worth, Texas, and was used to deliver new trailers to customers and dealerships. A few extra trouches were added to enhance the appearance, such as dual air horns, sun visor, radio and spot light. The new trailer being delivered is a Hobbs grain trailer. *Hobbs Trailer Co.*

This CO-190 was of the 1957 era. They were not the biggest tractors but they got the job done just as well. Its job was to pull this model SWX-12 Utility Spacemaster Van. With this 40-foot long, 13-foot, 6-inch high trailer, and the short wheelbase tractor, the rig was driveable in all states where a 50-foot length was the legal limit. The cast spoke wheels were standard equipment on most all International trucks, but this customer chose the optional disc wheels. *Utility Trailer Co.*

Many hauling companies used the popular Emeryville. This DCO-405 was used in a fleet that did a lot of heavy hauling of machinery and steel products. C&H Transportations Co. of Dallas, Texas, employed this tractor to pull the Loadcraft lowbed trailer. Notice all the license plates that were required at that time when traveling the lower 48 states. *C&H Transportation Co.*

Inland Motor Freight Inc. of Spokane, Washington, was not one of the bigger carriers, but they served the northwest area. They used a variety of different makes of equipment. One of those units was this DCO-405. Its 50-inch cab allowed it to pull this set of 25-foot Brown doubles at the 60-foot legal limit. The standard engine was the Cummins HRB-600 Diesel. *Inland Motor Freight*

The big super size RDF-405 was popular with owner/operators. Mr. Gillis Nelson of Wayne, Nebraska, was the owner of this RDF-405 that was leased to TransAmerican Freight Lines Inc. of Detroit, Michigan. When you look at the square refrigeration unit on the front of the trailer you can understand why the sleeper box had to be lowered in order to pull these kinds of reefer trailers. *Neil Sherff*

Navajo Freight Lines Inc., based at the Phoenix Terminal, owned these two AC-160 models. The AC-160 series had a GVW of 16,000 to 19,000 pounds. The only engine available in the AC-160 was the Black Diamond with 264 cubic inches. The wheelbases ranged from 125 to 189 inches. The van body is a Pike. *Navajo Freight Lines*

90

The "V" line models ranged from the 190 to the 230, the "V" being the four-wheel series and the "VF" being the six-wheel series. Here we see a VF-200 for Long Rodeo Co., owner Jack Long, of Kansas. The two engines offered were the V-461 and the V-549. The wheelbases ranged from 139 to 211. The VF-200 had a GVW of 37,000 pounds and a GCW of 65,000 pounds. A sleeper cab was available, but here the owner chose the add-on sleeper box. *Harry Patterson*

This ACF-220 was set up as a Midwest-type truck-trailer for steel hauling. The standard engine was a Cummins NH-180 Diesel. Owner D. Coffen chose the sleeper cab over the day cab. He leased his rig to the steel division of Yellow Transit Freight Lines Inc. of Indianapolis, Indiana. *Neil Sherff*

This DCO-405, 50-inch cab model was set up to pull double trailers, although only one is being pulled here. The Oregon Centennial is being commemorated on the side of this Reliance trailer. Oregon, Nevada, California (ONC) Fast Freight of San Carlos, California, is the owner of the rig. *O-N-C Fast Freight*

In February of 1958 the first sleeper cab was offered on the ACO-190, -200, and -220. It was a 72-inch cab and was well insulated. The cab tilted to service the V-401 engine. This one, with dual headlights, was leased to Ringle Express Inc. of Fowler, Indiana. This picture was taken in December of 1959 near Ypsilanti, Michigan. *Neil Sherff*

The ACO-225 was the heaviest in the 220 series. The GVW was 30,000 pounds with a GCW of 65,000 pounds. The standard engine is the V-461. The disc wheels were optional. This one is pulling a set of Utility doubles for the Boys Market. *Jack Jenkins*

This VCOF-195 was leased to Cushman Motor Delivery Co. of Chicago, Illinois. The rig is seen here hauling steel. Pulling the load was a V-401 gasoline engine. The cast spoke wheels were standard. *Neil Sherff*

The reason for the chicken crates is unknown, but at least this VCO-190 got a little bit of a boost. Bright Co-op Co. of Nacogdoches, Texas, was a hauler of wood products, produce, and grain in this Hobbs trailer. The standard engine was the V-401. The wheelbases for the VCO-190 went from 99 inches up to 203 inches. *Ron Adams Collection*

It is assumed that the unidentified gentlemen are two executives for Spector-Mid-States of Chicago, Illinois. This DCO-405 with Fruehauf reefer trailer was one in a fleet of several hundred trucks. The source of power was the Cummins HRB-600 Diesel. It had an 80-inch sleeper cab. *Spector-Mid-States*

International trucks came in handy for all kinds of uses. This DCOF-405 was doing duty in the California oilfields for BJ Oilfield Services Inc. of Long Beach, California. It used the 50-inch cab and had optional disc wheels. Little information is known about the truck, but whatever its function was I'm sure that it got the job done. *Ron Adams Collection*

This V-195 was kept busy traveling across country moving households for people on the move. The driver chose the Comfo-Vision sleeper cab for resting periods. Power came from the V-401 engine. The goods were hauled in the Highway moving van trailer. *Neil Sherff*

Here we have another V-190, but this time with an add-on sleeper box and pulling a Dorsey produce trailer. Many produce haulers used International trucks. *Harry Patterson*

The RDF-405 was International's big West Coast model. The available horsepower was anywhere from a 250 to a 335 Cummins Diesel. Mueller Truck Co. had this RDF-405 pulling a Trailmobile reefer trailer between San Diego and Los Angeles. Notice the jet plane over the top of the trailer. *Ron Adams Collection*

Midwest Emery Freight System Inc. of Chicago, Illinois, was a big refrigerated hauler from the Midwest to the East Coast. Their fleet consisted of both owner/operator and company owned tractors. This AC was one of the tractors in the black and yellow fleet pulling a Fruehauf reefer trailer. A Cummins Diesel powered it. It featured the standard cast spoke wheels and optional sleeper cab. *Neil Sherff*

This A-180 was owned by Kraft Foods and was based in Alabama. The A-180 came with the 282 Black Diamond engine but for heavier operations the 308-cubic-inch version was recommended. The body is an American with an Arctic Traveler refrigeration unit. *Scott Photography*

Another refrigerated carrier from the Midwest to the West Coast was Midwest Coast Transport Inc. of Sioux Falls, South Dakota. This DCOF-405 was one in the fleet pulling an American reefer trailer. A Cummins Diesel was the power source. This rig featured an 80-inch sleeper cab with the optional disc wheels. *Bill Day's Camera Shop*

Ephraim Freightways Inc. of Grand Junction, Colorado, made use of all the possible available space on this long wheelbase DCOF-405. It has an 80-inch sleeper cab and optional disc wheels. The trailer is a Fruehauf. Notice on the lower right corner of the dromedary body there is a cutout, which looks like the body could have been taken from another dromedary rig that was set up with twin steering axles. *Neil Sherff*

Crouch Bros. Inc. of St. Joseph, Missouri, seen here pulling a flatbed trailer, owned this ACOF Sightliner. It has the 48-inch cab, standard cast spoke wheels, and most likely the V-549 gasoline engine. The 48-inch cabs were short but there was plenty of room for comfort. The load contains International 460 tractors. *Crouch Bros. Inc.*

In 1959, the "turnpike trains" started to become a familiar sight on the turnpikes of Indiana, Ohio, the New York State thruway, and the Massachusetts turnpike. The standard engine for the job was the Cummins NRTO-335 Diesel. An option was the 817-cubic-inch International diesel. The GCW was around 127,000 pounds. Spector Freight System Inc. of Chicago, Illinois, was one of the companies that ventured into using the "turnpike trains." An 80-inch sleeper cab was chosen for this DCOF-405 tractor. These trains stretched out to around 97 feet depending on the wheelbase. *Ron Adams Collection*

Another company that used the turnpike train was Motor Cargo Inc. of Akron, Ohio. A team of drivers was piloting this DCF-405 on the Ohio turnpike on January 5, 1960. It's seen here pulling two Ohio 40-foot open-top trailers. This one features the old style 72-inch cab. *Henry M. Barr Photography*

Although the appearance looks nearly the same, a few changes were made. Dual headlights were new and recessed in the fender, and when the cab tilted, everything tilted. This DCO-405 had a 72-inch cab, but an 80-inch cab was available as an option. Wheelbases went from 137 to 212 inches. The engine in this one was the Cummins NRTO-6-B turbocharged that put out 335 horsepower. *International Harvester*

This DCOF-405 had the job of pulling the Heil milk tanker-trailer for William O'Donnel Inc. of Elkhorn, Wisconsin. It has a 54-inch cab and is powered by a Detroit Diesel. Although the Detroit Diesel did not arrive on the scene until 1961, this photo shows the day cab with the new appearance. Standard wheels were 20-inch cast spoke and options were 22-inch cast spoke or 20- and 22-inch disc wheels. *Detroit Diesel*

Another change in the lineup for 1959 was that the BC model replaced the AC model that had lasted only two years. Again, the appearance is similar to that of the AC except now there are dual headlights instead of singles. Navajo Freight Lines Inc. owned this BC-180. *Navajo Freight Lines*

This BCF-180 was hauling a high load of cargo-tainers. The engine was a V-345 Y-block V-8 as standard, and the wheelbases ranged from 125 to 238 inches. This truck was leased to the steel division of Yellow Transit Freight Lines Inc. of Indianapolis, Indiana. *Neil Sherff*

Another new series in 1959 was the B, which replaced the A series. The two noticeable changes were the egg crate grille and the vertical dual headlights. This one is equipped with a sleeper cab and is leased to Mayflower Transit Co. of Indianapolis, Indiana, pulling a Trailmobile moving van trailer. *Harry Patterson*

The B-170 was a lightweight tractor ready to do some medium size work. The Sanford Co. Inc. of Vernon, Alabama, manufactured roof trusses and hauled them on this Alabama drop deck trailer. The B-170 used a 15,000-pound rear axle. There were three 5-speed transmissions and a Select-O-Matic was also available. The company added dual air horns. *Ken Ives Studio and Alabama Trailer Co.*

Still being made in 1959 was this big RDF-405. There were six Cummins Diesels offered from 175 to 335 horsepower and 10 available transmissions. This one shows a chrome bumper, air horns, stack, and an aluminum sleeper box. This flying swan is flying high atop this big super size RDF-405 with a reefer trailer on behind. The carrier is unknown. *Neil Sherff*

A lot of short flatbed steel hauling trailers were used in the Michigan area. Here we have two loads of steel being pulled by a V-220 with a GVW of 26,000 pounds. Power came from the V-461 Y-block V-8. The optional engine was a V-549. The rig was leased to Hess Cartage Co. of Melvindale, Michigan. *Neil Sherff*

This model VF-195 Roadliner was kept busy hauling gasoline in the 8,385-gallon capacity Butler tank trailer owned by the Standard Oil Company. The V-401, V-461, and V-549 gasoline engines were offered. This side view shows the tractor with standard cast spoke wheels with optional sanders. A sleeper cab was also an option, although this one features the day cab. *Butler Steel Products*

The VCO-220 had the International V-478 gasoline V-8 engine, 23,000-pound rear axle, 5-speed transmission, and cast spoke wheels as standard. Wheelbases ranged from 99 to 203 inches. Optional sanders and grille guard were added. The Daitch Crystal Dairies Inc. of New York City, New York, owned this VCO-220 and Great Dane reefer trailer. *George Salkin Associates*

The RDF-405 made its way into the logging sites. They were big and tough enough to transport logs from site to mill. A Detroit Diesel, most likely a 318, powers this one. This one probably had the optional 15,000-pound front axle with optional disc wheels. *Detroit Diesel*

This somewhat fancied up Emeryville is transporting a load of steel and some other kind of flatbed product. This DCOF-405 was leased to the steel division for TransAmerican Freight Line Inc. of Detroit, Michigan. This one is of the newer style introduced in 1959. The engine is a standard Cummins and the rig has standard cast spoke wheels. *Neil Sherff*

Another sharp looking Emeryville is this DCOF-405. This one was selected to haul livestock for Chas. W. Wilkinson of Kike, Iowa. A number of chrome items, along with the fancy paint job, make this tractor stand out. The optional disc wheels were selected along with an 80-inch cab, seen here pulling a Wilson trailer. *Neil Sherff*

Midwest Haulers Inc. of Toledo, Ohio, ran from Ohio to the East Coast with a variety of different equipment. There were a good number of Internationals among the fleet, one of them being this BC-220. The standard for all models was the NH-180. For a heavier load, the NH-220 was recommended. For reasons unknown, the driver added covers atop each headlight and an extra bumper. *Neil Sherff*

One of the biggest users of Internationals was Navajo Freight Lines Inc. of Denver, Colorado. We see that the tractors were leased to General Expressways of Chicago, Illinois, who was also an International user. This was at the time when Navajo was taking over the operations of General. This was one of many DCOF-405s that traveled over the Navajo trails from coast to coast. This one featured a 72-inch standard cab and optional disc wheels. *Neil Sherff*

The products hauled in this rig are Pine-Sol and Perma starch. The appearance of this DCOF-405 and the 38-foot Dorsey reefer trailer makes a good-looking image not only for both manufacturers, but also for the Dumas-Milner Corp. of Jackson, Mississippi, and Illiopolis, Illinois. The standard cast spoke wheels were chosen and the tractor features the optional 80-inch cab. *Ron Adams Collection*

Here we have another BC-220 that is taking a break at Mac's Café. Stilwell Canning Co. Inc. of Stilwell, Oklahoma, is the owner of the diesel powered tractor and Fruehauf reefer and ventilated trailer. The cast spoke wheels were selected as standard and an optional sleeper cab was chosen. Notice the louvers on each side of the grille. This was probably for more airflow to cool the bigger engines like the NH-220. *Neil Sherff*

This CO-190 was a good truck for making store-to-store deliveries. The standard engine was the International RD-372 gasoline six. The transmission was a T-53 5-speed with overdrive. Wheelbases ranged from 99 to 203 inches. Van de Kamp's quality frozen food chose an ABC body with an Arctic Traveler refrigeration unit. *Aluminum Body Corp. (ABC)*

More Great Titles From Iconografix

TRUCKS

AM General: Hummers, Mutts, Buses & Postal Jeeps ISBN 1-58388-135-2
Autocar Trucks 1899-1950 Photo Archive ISBN 1-58388-115-8
Autocar Trucks 1950-1987 Photo Archive ISBN 1-58388-072-0
Beverage Trucks 1910-1975 Photo Archive ISBN 1-882256-60-3
*Brockway Trucks 1948-1961 Photo Archive** ISBN 1-882256-55-7
Chevrolet El Camino Photo History Incl. GMC Sprint & Caballero ISBN 1-58388-044-5
Circus and Carnival Trucks 1923-2000 Photo Archive ISBN 1-58388-048-8
Dodge B-Series Trucks Restorer's & Collector's Reference Guide and History ISBN 1-58388-087-9
Dodge C-Series Trucks Restorer's & Collector's Reference Guide and History ISBN 1-58388-140-9
Dodge Pickups 1939-1978 Photo Album ISBN 1-882256-82-4
Dodge Power Wagons 1940-1980 Photo Archive ISBN 1-882256-89-1
Dodge Power Wagon Photo History ISBN 1-58388-019-4
Dodge Ram Trucks 1994-2001 Photo History ISBN 1-58388-051-8
Dodge Trucks 1929-1947 Photo Archive ISBN 1-882256-36-0
Dodge Trucks 1948-1960 Photo Archive ISBN 1-882256-37-9
Ford 4x4s 1935-1990 Photo History ISBN 1-58388-079-8
Ford Heavy-Duty Trucks 1948-1998 Photo History ISBN 1-58388-043-7
Ford Medium-Duty Trucks 1917-1998 Photo History ISBN 1-58388-162-X
Ford Ranchero 1957-1979 Photo History ISBN 1-58388-126-3
Freightliner Trucks 1937-1981 Photo Archive ISBN 1-58388-090-9
FWD Trucks 1910-1974 Photo Archive ISBN 1-58388-142-5
GMC Heavy-Duty Trucks 1927-1987 ISBN 1-58388-125-5
International Heavy Trucks of the 1950s: At Work ISBN 1-58388-160-3
International Heavy Trucks of the 1960s: At Work ISBN 1-58388-161-1
Jeep 1941-2000 Photo Archive ISBN 1-58388-021-6
Jeep Prototypes & Concept Vehicles Photo Archive ISBN 1-58388-033-X
Kenworth Trucks 1950-1979 At Work ISBN 1-58388-147-6
*Mack Model AB Photo Archive** ISBN 1-882256-18-2
*Mack AP Super-Duty Trucks 1926-1938 Photo Archive** ISBN 1-882256-54-9
*Mack Model B 1953-1966 Volume 2 Photo Archive** ISBN 1-882256-34-4
*Mack EB-EC-ED-EE-EF-EG-DE 1936-1951 Photo Archive** ISBN 1-882256-29-8
*Mack FC-FCSW-NW 1936-1947 Photo Archive** ISBN 1-882256-28-X
*Mack FG-FH-FJ-FK-FN-FP-FT-FW 1937-1950 Photo Archive** ISBN 1-882256-35-2
*Mack LF-LH-LJ-LM-LT 1940-1956 Photo Archive** ISBN 1-882256-38-7
*Mack Trucks Photo Gallery** ISBN 1-882256-88-3
New Car Carriers 1910-1998 Photo Album ISBN 1-882256-98-0
Peterbilt Trucks 1939-1979 At Work ISBN 1-58388-152-2
Refuse Trucks Photo Archive ISBN 1-58388-042-9
Studebaker Trucks 1927-1940 Photo Archive ISBN 1-882256-40-9
White Trucks 1900-1937 Photo Archive ISBN 1-882256-80-8

RAILWAYS

Burlington Zephyrs Photo Archive: America's Distinctive Trains ISBN 1-58388-124-7
Chicago & North Western Passenger Trains of the 400 Fleet Photo Archive ISBN 1-58388-159-X
Chicago, St. Paul, Minneapolis & Omaha Railway 1880-1940 Photo Archive ISBN 1-882256-67-0
Classic Sreamliners Photo Archive: The Trains and the Designers ISBN 1-58388-144-x
Freight Trains of the Upper Mississippi River Photo Archive ISBN 1-58388-136-0
Great Northern Railway 1945-1970 Volume 2 Photo Archive ISBN 1-882256-79-4
Great Northern Railway Ore Docks of Lake Superior Photo Archive ISBN 1-58388-073-9
Illinois Central Railroad 1854-1960 Photo Archive ISBN 1-58388-063-1
Locomotives of the Upper Midwest Photo Archive: Diesel Power in the 1960s and 1970s ISBN 1-58388-113-1
Milwaukee Road 1850-1960 Photo Archive ISBN 1-882256-61-1
Milwaukee Road Depots 1856-1954 Photo Archive ISBN 1-58388-040-2
Show Trains of the 20th Century ISBN 1-58388-030-5
Soo Line 1975-1992 Photo Archive ISBN 1-882256-68-9
Steam Locomotives of the B&O Railroad Photo Archive ISBN 1-58388-095-X
Streamliners to the Twin Cities Photo Archive 400, Twin Zephyrs & Hiawatha Trains ISBN 1-58388-096-8
Trains of the Twin Ports Photo Archive, Duluth-Superior in the 1950s ISBN 1-58388-003-8
Trains of the Circus 1872-1956 ISBN 1-58388-024-0
Trains of the Upper Midwest Photo Archive Steam & Diesel in the 1950s & 1960s ISBN 1-58388-036-4

All Iconografix books are available from direct mail specialty book dealers and bookstores worldwide, or can be ordered from the publisher. For book trade and distribution information or to add your name to our mailing list and receive a **FREE CATALOG** contact:

Iconografix, Inc.
PO Box 446, Dept BK
Hudson, WI, 54016

Telephone: (715) 381-9755,
(800) 289-3504 (USA),
Fax: (715) 381-9756
info@iconografixinc.com
www.iconografixinc.com

*This product is sold under license from Mack Trucks, Inc. Mack is a registered Trademark of Mack Trucks, Inc. All rights reserved.

BUSES

Buses of ACF Photo Archive Including ACF-Brill And CCF-Brill ISBN 1-58388-101-8
Buses of Motor Coach Industries 1932-2000 Photo Archive ISBN 1-58388-039-9
City Transit Buses of the 20th Century Photo Gallery ISBN 1-58388-146-8
Fageol & Twin Coach Buses 1922-1956 Photo Archive ISBN 1-58388-075-5
Flxible Intercity Buses 1924-1970 Photo Archive ISBN 1-58388-108-5
Flxible Transit Buses 1953-1995 Photo Archive ISBN 1-58388-053-4
GM Intercity Coaches 1944-1980 Photo Archive ISBN 1-58388-099-2
Greyhound in Postcards: Buses, Depots and Posthouses ISBN 1-58388-130-1
Highway Buses of the 20th Century Photo Gallery ISBN 1-58388-121-2
*Mack® Buses 1900-1960 Photo Archive** ISBN 1-58388-020-8
New York City Transit Buses 1945-1975 Photo Archive ISBN 1-58388-149-2
Prevost Buses 1924-2002 Photo Archive ISBN 1-58388-083-6
Trailways Buses 1936-2001 Photo Archive ISBN 1-58388-029-1
Trolley Buses 1913-2001 Photo Archive ISBN 1-58388-057-7
Welcome Aboard the GM New Look Bus: An Enthusiast's Reference ISBN 1-58388-167-0
Yellow Coach Buses 1923-1943 Photo Archive ISBN 1-58388-054-2

EMERGENCY VEHICLES

100 Years of American LaFrance: An Illustrated History ISBN 1-58388-139-5
The American Ambulance 1900-2002: An Illustrated History ISBN 1-58388-081-X
American Fire Apparatus Co. 1922-1993 Photo Archive ISBN 1-58388-131-X
American Funeral Vehicles 1883-2003 Illustrated History ISBN 1-58388-104-2
American LaFrance 700 Series 1945-1952 Photo Archive ISBN 1-882256-90-5
American LaFrance 700 Series 1945-1952 Photo Archive Volume 2 ISBN 1-58388-025-9
American LaFrance 700 & 800 Series 1953-1958 Photo Archive ISBN 1-882256-91-3
American LaFrance 900 Series 1958-1964 Photo Archive ISBN 1-58388-002-X
Classic Seagrave 1935-1951 Photo Archive ISBN 1-58388-034-8
Crown Firecoach 1951-1985 Photo Archive ISBN 1-58388-047-X
Elevating Platforms: A Fire Apparatus Photo Gallery ISBN 1-58388-164-6
Encyclopedia of Canadian Fire Apparatus ISBN 1-58388-119-0
Fire Chief Cars 1900-1997 Photo Album ISBN 1-882256-87-5
Firefighting Tanker Trucks and Tenders: A Fire Apparatus Photo Gallery ISBN 1-58388-138-7
FWD Fire Trucks 1914-1963 Photo Archive ISBN 1-58388-156-5
Grumman Fire Apparatus 1976-1992 Photo Archive ISBN 1-58388-165-4
Hahn Fire Apparatus 1923-1990 Photo Archive ISBN 1-58388-077-1
Heavy Rescue Trucks 1931-2000 Photo Gallery ISBN 1-58388-045-3
Imperial Fire Apparatus 1969-1976 Photo Archive ISBN 1-58388-091-7
Industrial and Private Fire Apparatus 1925-2001 Photo Archive ISBN 1-58388-049-6
*Mack Model L Fire Trucks 1940-1954 Photo Archive** ISBN 1-882256-86-7
Mack Fire Trucks 1911-2005 Illustrated History ISBN 1-58388-157-3
Maxim Fire Apparatus 1914-1989 Photo Archive ISBN 1-58388-050-X
Maxim Fire Apparatus Photo History ISBN 1-58388-111-5
Navy & Marine Corps Fire Apparatus 1836 -2000 Photo Gallery ISBN 1-58388-031-3
Pierre Thibault Ltd. Fire Apparatus 1918-1990 Photo Archive ISBN 1-58388-074-7
Pirsch Fire Apparatus 1890-1991 Photo Archive ISBN 1-58388-082-8
Police Cars: Restoring, Collecting & Showing America's Finest Sedans ISBN 1-58388-046-1
Saulsbury Fire Rescue Apparatus 1956-2003 Photo Archive ISBN 1-58388-106-9
Seagrave 70th Anniversary Series Photo Archive ISBN 1-58388-001-1
Seagrave Fire Apparatus 1959-2004 Photo Archive ISBN 1-58388-132-8
TASC Fire Apparatus 1946-1985 Photo Archive ISBN 1-58388-065-8
Van Pelt Fire Apparatus 1925-1987 Photo Archive ISBN 1-58388-143-3
Volunteer & Rural Fire Apparatus Photo Gallery ISBN 1-58388-005-4
W.S. Darley & Co. Fire Apparatus 1908-2000 Photo Archive ISBN 1-58388-061-5
Wildland Fire Apparatus 1940-2001 Photo Gallery ISBN 1-58388-056-9
Young Fire Equipment 1932-1991 Photo Archive ISBN 1-58388-015-1

RECREATIONAL VEHICLES & OTHER

Commercial Ships on the Great Lakes Photo Gallery ISBN 1-58388-153-0
Phillips 66 1945-1954 Photo Archive ISBN 1-882256-42-5
RVs & Campers 1900-2000: An Illustrated History ISBN 1-58388-064-X
Ski-Doo Racing Sleds 1960-2003 Photo Archive ISBN 1-58388-105-0
The Collector's Guide to Ski-Doo Snowmobiles ISBN 1-58388-133-6

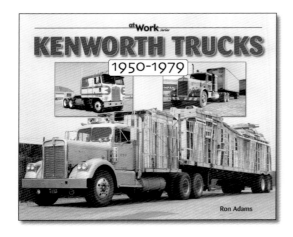

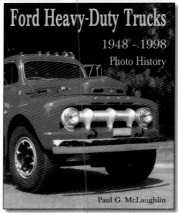

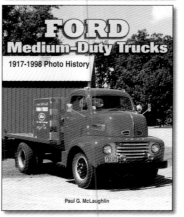